# BRIGHT IDEA BOOKS

# LUNGLESS
# Salamanders

by Emily Hudd

**Content Consultant**

Gian L. Rocco
Project Manager/Wildlife Biologist
Western EcoSystems Technology

CAPSTONE PRESS
a capstone imprint

Bright Idea Books are published by Capstone Press
1710 Roe Crest Drive, North Mankato, Minnesota 56003
www.mycapstone.com

**Library of Congress Cataloging-in-Publication Data**
Names: Hudd, Emily, author.
Title: Lungless salamanders / by Emily Hudd.
Description: North Mankato, Minnesota : Capstone Press, [2020] | Series:
   Unique animal adaptations | Audience: Grade 4 to 6. | Includes
   bibliographical references and index.
Identifiers: LCCN 2018061084 (print) | LCCN 2019000097 (ebook) | ISBN
   9781543571745 (ebook) | ISBN 9781543571547 (hardcover) | ISBN 9781543575088 (paperback)
Subjects: LCSH: Lungless salamanders--Juvenile literature. | Lungless
   salamanders--Adaptation--Juvenile literature.
Classification: LCC QL668.C274 (ebook) | LCC QL668.C274 H83 2020 (print) |
   DDC 597.8/59--dc23
LC record available at https://lccn.loc.gov/2018061084

All internet sites appearing in back matter were available and accurate when this book was sent to press.

**Editorial Credits**
Editor: Marie Pearson
Designer: Becky Daum
Production Specialist: Colleen McLaren

**Photo Credits**
Newscom: Rauschenbach, F./picture alliance/Arco Images G, 14; Shutterstock Images: Federico. Crovetto, 6–7, 17, 29, Frank Reiser, 21, Jason Patrick Ross, 22–23, Jay Ondreicka, cover, 5, 9, 12–13, 18–19, 25, 28, 30–31, Nashepard, 10, Oliver Fahle, 27

Design Elements: Red Line Editorial

Printed in the United States of America.
PA70

# TABLE OF CONTENTS

# CHAPTER 1

# LUNGLESS Salamanders

See that long, glossy creature under the rock? It is a lungless salamander! Lungless salamanders are amphibians. Amphibians can breathe through their skin.

Lungless salamanders have smooth skin. They can be red or orange. They can be brown or gray. Black spots may cover their skin.

Lungless salamanders come in many colors.

Most lungless salamanders are small. Their heads and bodies are 1.5 to 5 inches (4 to 12 centimeters) long. Each salamander has four legs and a tail. The tail is longer than the body. Sometimes it is twice as long as the body.

## SHORT LEGS

Lungless salamanders' legs are very short. Their bellies drag on the ground when they walk!

There are more than 250 **species** of lungless salamanders. Most live in North and South America. Many live in forests. They crawl on the ground. They live in **habitats** with water.

A forest has shade and water for lungless salamanders.

# CHAPTER 2

# ADAPTATIONS

Lungless salamanders have **adapted** to their environment. Most animals need oxygen to live. Oxygen is a gas. It gives the body energy. Many animals breathe oxygen with their lungs. But lungless salamanders do not have lungs. They breathe through their skin. Lungs fill with air. This would make their bodies float in water. So they have adapted to breathe without lungs.

These animals dive into the water to catch food. They hide on the bottom of streams or under rocks to escape predators.

Lungless salamanders use their skin to breathe.

Lungless salamanders need wet skin to breathe. The skin **absorbs** oxygen from the air and water. Too much wind or sunshine can dry the skin. Then the animals can't breathe.

Lungless salamanders use their mouths to help them breathe.

The salamanders also breathe through a **lining** in the mouth. The lining flutters to move the air. It pulls in oxygen from the air.

## CAVE SPECIES

Some species of salamanders live in caves. Their bodies change as they grow. They adapt to the dark habitat. Their skin loses color. Their eyes disappear. Their eyelids close up.

# SPECIAL BODIES

Lungless salamanders' bodies cannot create heat. They cannot sweat to cool off. They use the environment. They lie in the sun to warm up. They find shade under rocks or plants to stay cool.

Some lungless salamanders eat insects.

Salamanders do not have ears. They can't hear sounds. Some have sensitive bodies. They can feel **vibrations**.

Some salamanders have strong tongues. They flick them when food gets close. Their tongues catch small worms and insects.

# CHAPTER 3

# LIFE Cycle

**Female** lungless salamanders lay eggs. One female can lay 1 to 450 eggs. Some lay eggs on land or underwater. They place the eggs in **moss** or under rocks. Then they guard the eggs.

# PROTECTING EGGS

Females have different ways of protecting their eggs. Some put their bodies around the eggs. Some wrap leaves around them. The eggs stay hidden.

Females protect their eggs until they hatch.

Gills grow from a larva's neck.

18

After a few weeks, the young salamanders hatch. Some hatch with their adult form. But most hatch as **larvae**. They have four legs and a tail. They look like tiny adults. But they have **gills**. They live in water.

Larvae eat tiny insects and plants that float in the water. They don't eat the same food as the adults. This helps them survive.

Larvae grow and change. Their bodies get bigger. Their gills disappear. Some become adults in just three months. Others aren't adults until they are more than four years old. Many leave the water. They live on land.

Lungless salamander larvae sometimes eat mosquito larvae (pictured).

# DAILY LIFE

Salamanders are active at any time of day. They are most active when it rains. When it is dry, they dig into the ground. The **moist** soil helps them stay wet.

**Multiple lungless salamanders live in the same area.**

Lungless salamanders live in groups. Most live for about 10 years. Adults live in the same area their whole lives.

# CHAPTER 4

# STAYING Safe

Big animals eat lungless salamanders. Salamanders have to be careful. They do not have tough skin. Hiding is their best **defense**. They hide under things or in small spaces.

Hiding is one way lungless salamanders stay safe.

Clean environments help lungless salamanders survive. Trees shade the ground. Plants keep the soil moist and healthy. Most importantly, salamanders need water. People help them survive by taking care of the environment.

Scientists study lungless salamanders to learn how to help them survive.

# GLOSSARY

**absorb**
to take in

**adapt**
to have differences that help a species fit into a new or different environment

**defense**
how an animal protects itself

**female**
an animal of the sex that can lay eggs or have babies

**gill**
an organ that helps an animal breathe in water

**habitat**
the place where an animal lives

**larva**
a baby salamander that hatches from an egg and has a different body than adults; the plural is larvae

**lining**
a thin layer of skin

**moist**
a little wet and not dry

**moss**
a type of plant that is soft and wet

**species**
a specific type of animal

**vibration**
a small movement carried through the ground or air

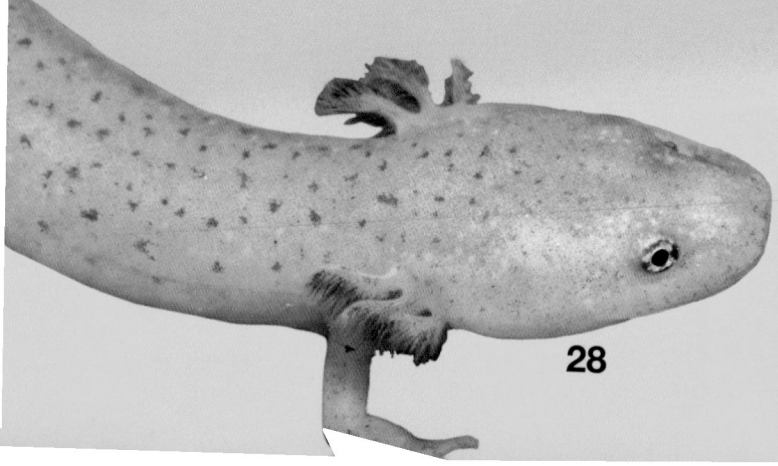

# TRIVIA

1. Lungless salamanders adapted to water habitats by learning to breathe without lungs.

2. Female lungless salamanders can lay up to 450 eggs.

3. Lungless salamanders are more active when it rains.

4. Lungless salamanders belong to the scientific family Plethodontidae.

# ACTIVITY

# STAYING MOIST

Imagine you needed moist skin like a lungless salamander. Write a paragraph about how you would keep from drying out. What conditions might dry out your skin? Where could you go if you needed to make your skin moist? What places would you have to avoid or risk drying out?

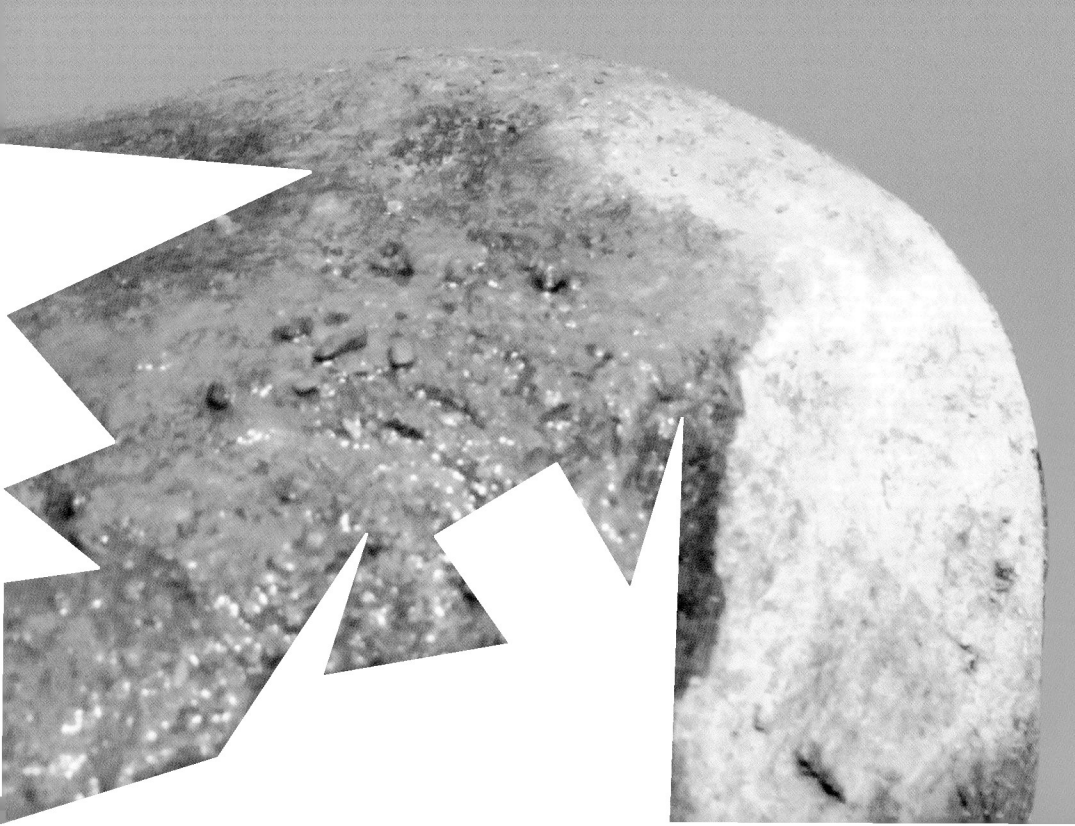

# FURTHER RESOURCES

## Amazed by salamanders? Learn more here:

Gish, Melissa. *Salamanders*. Living Wild. Mankato, Minn.: Creative Education, 2018.

Guillain, Charlotte. *Life Story of a Salamander*. Animal Life Stories. Chicago, Ill: Heinemann Library, 2015.

San Diego Zoo: Salamander and Newt
https://animals.sandiegozoo.org/animals/salamander-and-newt

## Ready to learn about other amphibians? Check out these resources:

Mattison, Chris. *Reptiles and Amphibians*. New York: DK Publishing, 2017.

National Geographic Kids: Amphibians
https://kids.nationalgeographic.com/animals/hubs/amphibians/

San Diego Zoo: Amphibians
https://animals.sandiegozoo.org/animals/amphibians

# INDEX